SCHOLASTIC

C000148641

writing gu...

With interactive resources on CD-ROM

News Stories

for ages 7-9

Huw Thomas

Credits

Author and Series Consultant
Huw Thomas

Development Editor
Simret Brar

Editor
Liz Dalby

Series Designer
Anna Oliwa

Designer
Paul Stockmans

Cover Illustration
Mark Oliver

Illustrations
Michael Rees

CD-ROM Development
CD-ROM developed in association with Infuze Ltd

Book layout
Quadrum Solutions Ltd

Mixed Sources
Product group from well-managed forests and other controlled sources
www.fsc.org Cert no. TT-COC-002769
© 1996 Forest Stewardship Council
FSC

Text © Huw Thomas
© 2010 Scholastic Ltd

Designed using Adobe InDesign

Published by Scholastic Ltd,
Book End,
Range Road,
Witney,
Oxfordshire
OX29 0YD

www.scholastic.co.uk

Printed by Bell & Bain

1 2 3 4 5 6 7 8 9   0 1 2 3 4 5 6 7 8

British Library Cataloguing-in-Publication Data
A catalogue record for this book is available from the British Library.

ISBN 978-1407-11258-9

Acknowledgments
Mirror Group for the use of headlines and extracts from *The Mirror* © 1998, 1999, 2001, Mirrorpix.com (1998, 1999, 2001, *The Mirror*)

CD-ROM Minimum specifications:

Windows 2000/XP/Vista	Mac OSX 10.4	
Processor: 1 GHz	RAM: 512 MB	Graphics card: 32bit
Audio card: Yes	CD-ROM drive speed: 8x	Hard disk space: 200MB
Screen resolution: 800x600		

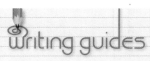

Contents

Introduction: News Stories

The *Writing Guides* series aims to inspire and motivate children as writers by using creative approaches. Each *Writing Guide* contains activities and photocopiable resources designed to develop children's understanding of a particular genre (for example, fairy stories). The activities are in line with the requirements of the National Curriculum and the recommendations in the *Primary Framework for Literacy*. The teacher resource books are accompanied by a CD-ROM containing a range of interactive activities and resources.

What's in the book?

The *Writing Guides* series provides a structured approach to developing children's writing. Each book is divided into four sections.

Section 1: **Using good examples**
Three text extracts are provided to explore the typical features of the genre.

Section 2: **Developing writing**
There are ten short, focussed writing tasks in this section. These are designed to develop children's ability to use the key features of the genre in their own writing. The teacher's notes explain the objective of each activity and provide guidance on delivery, including how to use the photocopiable pages and the materials on the CD-ROM.

Section 3: **Writing**
The three writing projects in this section require the children to produce an extended piece of writing using the key features of the genre.

Section 4: **Review**
This section consists of a 'Self review', 'Peer review' and 'Teacher review'. These can be used to evaluate how effectively the children have met the writing criteria for the genre.

What's on the CD-ROM?

The accompanying CD-ROM contains a range of motivating activities and resources. The activities can be used for independent work or can be used on an interactive whiteboard to enhance group teaching.
Each CD-ROM contains:

- three text extracts that illustrate the typical features of the genre
- interactive versions of selected photocopiable pages
- four photographs and an audio file to create imaginative contexts for writing
- a selection of writing templates and images which can be used to produce extended pieces of writing.

The interactive activities on the CD-ROM promote active learning and support a range of teaching approaches and learning styles. For example, drag and drop and sequencing activities will support kinaesthic learners.

Talk for writing

Each *Writing Guide* uses the principles of 'Talk for writing' to support children's writing development by providing opportunities for them to rehearse ideas orally in preparation for writing. 'Talk for writing' is promoted using a variety of teaching strategies including discussions, questioning and drama activities (such as, developing imaginative dialogue – see *Fantasy Stories for Ages 9–11*).

How to use the CD-ROM

Start screen: click on the 'Start' button to go to the main menu.

This section contains brief instructions on how to use the CD-ROM. For more detailed guidance, go to 'How to use the CD-ROM' on the start screen or click on the 'Help' button located in the top right-hand corner of the screen.

Installing the CD-ROM

Follow the instructions on the disk to install the CD-ROM onto your computer. Once the CD-ROM is installed, navigate to the program location and double click on the program icon to open it.

Main menu screen

Main menu

The main menu provides links to all of the writing activities and resources on the CD-ROM. Clicking on a button from the main menu will take you to a sub-menu that lists all of the activities and resources in that section. From here you have the option to 'Launch' the interactive activities, which may contain more than one screen, or print out the activities for pupils to complete by hand.

If you wish to return to a previous menu, click the 'Menu' button in the top right-hand corner of the screen; this acts as a 'back' button.

Screen tools

A range of simple writing tools that can be used in all of the writing activities are contained in the toolbar at the bottom of the screen.

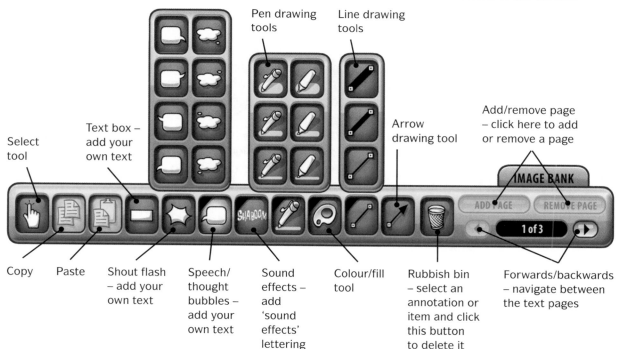

Pen drawing tools

Line drawing tools

Select tool

Text box – add your own text

Arrow drawing tool

Add/remove page – click here to add or remove a page

Copy

Paste

Shout flash – add your own text

Speech/ thought bubbles – add your own text

Sound effects – add 'sound effects' lettering

Colour/fill tool

Rubbish bin – select an annotation or item and click this button to delete it

Forwards/backwards – navigate between the text pages

How to use the CD-ROM

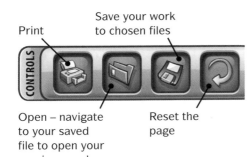

Print

Save your work to chosen files

Open – navigate to your saved file to open your previous work

Reset the page

Printing and saving work

All of the resources on the CD-ROM are printable. You can also save and retrieve any annotations made on the writing activities. Click on the 'Controls' tab on the right-hand side of the screen to access the 'Print', 'Open', 'Save' and 'Reset screen' buttons.

View all thumbnails by clicking on the arrows

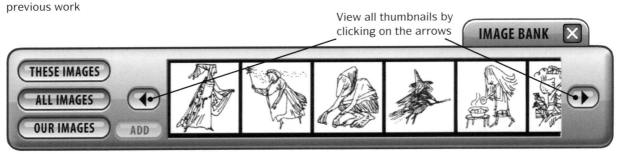

IMAGE BANK

THESE IMAGES

ALL IMAGES

OUR IMAGES

ADD

Image bank – click and drag an image to add it to an activity

Image bank

Each CD-ROM has an 'Image bank' containing images appropriate to the genre being taught. Click on the tab at the bottom right of the screen to open the 'Image bank'. On the left-hand side there are three large buttons.

- The 'These images' button will display only the images associated with the specific activity currently open.
- The 'All images' button will display all the photographs and illustrations available on the CD-ROM.
- The 'Our images' button will contain any images you or the children have added to the CD-ROM.

Press the left or right arrows to scroll through the images available. Select an image and drag and drop it into the desired location on the screen. If necessary, resize the image using the arrow icon that appears at the bottom right of the image.

You can upload images to the 'Image bank', including digital photographs or images drawn and scanned into the computer. Click on 'Our images' and then 'Add' to navigate to where the image is stored. A thumbnail picture will be added to the gallery.

Writing your own story

Each CD-ROM contains a selection of blank writing templates. The fiction genre templates will be categorised under the button 'My story' and the non-fiction templates will be categorised under 'My recount' or 'My writing'. The writing templates encourage the children to produce an extended piece of genre writing. They can also add images, speech bubbles and use other tools to enhance their work.

The fiction titles also include a cover template for the children to use. They can customise their cover by adding their own title, blurb and images.

Section 1

Using good examples

Using news stories

The examples in this section provide a way into the genre, with certain features that should be highlighted. The activities facilitate analysis and understanding of aspects of news writing. The main features to look out for are:

- Interest: Looking at current events; whether these are big, historic or small events, look for newsworthy events that grab our interest. Some events are of national or international significance while others will be small-scale human interest stories.

- Variety and range: For example, comparing and contrasting the front pages of tabloid and broadsheet newspapers. There is a likelihood that the stories in each type of newspaper vary, catering for the specific readers that the papers are aimed at.

- Headlines: Looking at how headlines draw the reader in, considering the wordplay and how headlines are constructed is vital. Headlines can announce momentous occasions to startling facts.

- Details and facts: As you look through the examples in this section you will see that journalists are constantly answering the basic questions about a news story: Who? What? When? Where? Why? Readers want to know the facts and the details. However, part of the craft of news writing is to do this with brevity. In the examples there are instances of facts being effectively communicated, often within the first line of the story. This is a habit to point out, highlight and cultivate.

- Insight: News stories can take us to the situation they report. One vital tool is the quote. As readers we don't just want the facts, we also want to hear what the people involved in the story are feeling.

- Interesting stories: It is really important that the class start to build up their own portfolio of interesting news stories. You can do this by asking them to seek out stories that can be used alongside the materials that follow.

News story features

Audience
- Story is of interest to the reader.

Structure
- Details give facts of the story.
- Use of quotations.

Content
- Who? What? When? Where? Why?

Style
- Headlines grab the reader's attention.
- Writing is edited down for brevity.

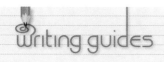

Extract 1: Note-able discovery

What's on the CD-ROM

Extract: Note-able discovery
- Text to display and share with the class.

Annotated news
- Text entry and roll over activity. Good news writing starts with questioning and investigating. The activity extends the questions to show the breadth of enquiry behind a good story.

Analyse a report that presents a model of news reporting.

- Display the article on photocopiable page 10 and read it through with the children. Ask them how it is different from other types of writing. Gather some examples and then, noting the headline, read the opening paragraph.

- Explain to the children that good news reporting answers the basic questions: Who? What? When? Where? Why?

- Point out that even if they only read this first paragraph they would have the basic facts of the whole story. Explain that news stories are often cut from the end in order to fit the space available, and readers often only read the first part of a news story.

- Highlight the quotes in the story, asking the children to read them aloud. Ask why they think these are used in the story. (They provide an insight into how those involved felt.) What do they add to the facts? (They provide an outlet for opinions.) Tell the children to re-read the story, imagining they are a newspaper editor. Why would they run a story like this? What makes it interesting? (The rarity of the event, human interest.)

- Open the activity 'Annotated news' on the CD-ROM; ask the children to review the way 'Note-able discovery' contains the various features discussed in shared reading.

Extract 2: These are the headlines

What's on the CD-ROM

Extract: These are the headlines
- Text to display and share with the class.

Alternative headlines
- Drag and drop the alternative headlines to match the news stories.

This lesson looks at a selection of headlines and opening sentences helping the children to focus on the very start of a newspaper story.

- Ask the children if they know what a headline is and what job it does in a news story. You could refer to 'Note-able discovery' as an example.

- Show the class the headlines from photocopiable page 11 'These are the headlines'; with each of the first paragraphs covered up, ask them to guess what each story is about. Make a list of the children's suggestions, then reveal the opening sentences and check how well they guessed.

- Talk about wordplay in some of the headlines. The children may need support in working out the references. Are the headlines funny? Would any of the headlines make them want to read more?

- Open the activity 'Alternative headlines' on the CD-ROM. Ask the children to place their favourite alternative headlines above each story.

- Look again at the opening paragraphs. Recap how the complete story is summarised in the opening paragraph and how the rest of a news story is elaboration of detail, comment and quotation.

Extract 3: One small step

What's on the CD-ROM

Extract: One small step
- Editable extract to display and discuss.

Comparing news
- Text entry activity that takes a story and compares it with the coverage of others.

Media resources
- Image of 'Buzz Aldrin' landing on the moon to discuss.

This lesson helps children identify the main features in a news story and asks them to compare other stories against this criteria.

- Display the image of Buzz Aldrin, on the moon and ask the children why they think this event was so important and newsworthy.

- Read through the news story 'One small step' with the class. Ask them if they have any thoughts about what makes it an effective piece of news reporting. The children can edit this story at the end of the lesson.

- Hand out copies of photocopiable page 16 'News story' and explain that the features in the first column are ones they will be looking for in news that they read.

- Ask the children to re-read 'One small step', finding ways in which it meets the criteria on the grid. They can note these down in the first column.

- Look at two other news stories for comparison so that the children can complete the sheet.

- Put the children in small groups and open the activity 'Comparing news' on the CD-ROM. Give each group four stories to compare and ask them to fill out the activity on screen.

- Compare the news stories and ask the children which they think has been the most effective at doing its task of communicating the news, and why. Challenge them to add or change bits of extract 3 to improve on it.

Poster: In the news

What's on the CD-ROM

In the news
- The features children will need throughout news writing are displayed on the poster, and the interactive version gives some additional questions to be applied to news stories, by rolling over the text.

The poster on page 18 can be used throughout any of the news-writing projects. It is best used alongside examples of news stories that children bring in, as well as the ones in this section. Display the poster where the class can see it for reference.

- Ask each child to bring in a story from a newspaper. Share these and look at whether any of the children have the same news item but from different papers. Was the story covered differently?

- Look at the poster on the CD-ROM and ask the children why the stories they brought in were of interest to them. Was it the writing style? The headline? The photograph?

- Check the details in the news stories. Encourage them to audit their text for answers to the questions on the poster: Who? What? When? Where? Why? Has the writer packed in detail? Are quotes used? If so, what do they add?

- Ask the children to rank the headlines to find the class's three favourite headlines out of all their examples. What do they think makes these headlines work?

Note-able discovery

A GIRL'S message in a bottle was picked up 600 miles away by the Swedish cousin of her school classmate.

Kaylee Richards' note was found on a beach by Camilla Larsson, 13, two years after it was sent.

But now Kaylee, 11, and Camilla – who began writing to each other – have discovered a mutual acquaintance.

A letter from Camilla said she had two cousins, Amelia and Christopher, who lived in England.

Kaylee sat next to a girl in primary school called Amelia – and remembered her brother was Christopher.

She told Camilla and heard back: "Amelia IS my cousin and she has told me all about you."

Kaylee, from Longbenton, Newcastle-upon-Tyne, said: "Now I'd love it if we could all get together."

Her father Michael, 46, added: "This must be a million-to-one chance, an incredible coincidence."

Text © 1999, Mirror Group.

The Mirror, 4th October 1999

These are the headlines

Dogs are left £30m

AN aristocrat has left his £30million fortune to his only friends – his dogs.

The Mirror, 6th June 1998

FLAMING DAY OFF

A FIREMAN who has never tackled a blaze in 29 years missed out when flames finally flared – on his day off.

The Mirror, 24th November 1999

Yes... peas in our time

By AIDAN McGURRAN

PEAS are to stay on a restaurant chain's menu by popular demand.

The Mirror, 6th June 2001

DOG SURVIVES 140FT PLUNGE

By RICHARD WHITE

HENRY the retriever escaped with just an injured paw after plunging 140ft from a cliff top.

The Mirror, 3rd October 2001

21st July 1969

DAILY NEWS

ONE SMALL STEP

Armstrong takes first step on surface of the moon. At 3.56 this morning, history was made when Neil Armstrong, one of the astronauts on the Apollo 11 mission, took a first step onto the moon.

In an event that is seen as the culmination of the historic race to put a person on the moon, Armstrong, along with fellow astronaut Edwin 'Buzz' Aldrin landed their fragile craft, called the Eagle, on the moon's surface in a place called 'The Sea of Tranquillity'. The third member of the Apollo team, Mike Collins, continues to orbit the moon, waiting for the return of his two colleagues. Their successful landing was announced at to a waiting world with the signal 'The Eagle has landed'.

There had been concerns at mission control in Houston about the fuel levels in the lunar module, one controller responded "We've got a bunch of guys on the ground about to turn blue." After a short rest period the astronauts opened the hatch on their craft and Armstrong descended to the moon, announcing "That's one small step for a man, one giant leap for mankind."

Aldrin joined Armstrong on the surface of the moon, describing the landscape as 'magnificent desolation'. The pair planted a United States flag on the surface and then took part in a telephone conversation with the President of the United States. During the

telephone call President Nixon said "this certainly has to be the most historic telephone call ever made".

The landing was watched by a worldwide audience of 600 million viewers. Many world leaders have congratulated the astronauts on their heroic achievement, including the British Prime Minister. Mr Wilson described this as "a most historic scientific achievement".

Read more inside: pages 2,3,4,5 and 6

Illustration © 2010, Michael Rees

Section 1: Using good examples

Annotated news

Headline

How does the headline use words in a clever way?

_____

_____

_____

First paragraph

What questions are answered in this paragraph?

_____

_____

_____

Details

How many details can you find in this story?

_____

_____

_____

_____

Quotes

Who is quoted and how do they feature in the story?

_____

_____

Note-able discovery

A GIRL'S message in a bottle was picked up 600 miles away by the Swedish cousin of her school classmate.

Kaylee Richards' note was found on a beach by Camilla Larsson, 13, two years after it was sent.

But now Kaylee, 11, and Camilla – who began writing to each other – have discovered a mutual acquaintance.

A letter from Camilla said she had two cousins, Amelia and Christopher, who lived in England.

Kaylee sat next to a girl in primary school called Amelia – and remembered her brother was Christopher.

She told Camilla and heard back: "Amelia IS my cousin and she has told me all about you."

Kaylee, from Longbenton, Newcastle-upon-Tyne, said: "Now I'd love it if we could all get together."

Her father Michael, 46, added: "This must be a million-to-one chance, an incredible coincidence."

The Mirror, 4th October 1999

Text © 1999, Mirror Group.

Alternative headlines

DOG SURVIVES

Hot Dogs

WHAT THE BLAZES?

Bark to Bank

PEAS-FUL MENU

Fireman has problems

RESTAURANT CHANGES MENU

LUCKY DOGS

You're Fired

FIRE! FIRE!

Flying Dog

Rich Dogs

Pea-Po!

DOG DIVING

BARKING MAD

Peas are back

UNFROZEN PEAS

WOOF WOOF MILLIONAIRES

Day off, off

30 MILLION DOGS

Section 1: Using good examples

News story

- Use this grid to find features of three news stories.

	News story 1	News story 2	News story 3
What makes this story interesting?			
How does the headline introduce the story?			
What questions does it answer?			
Can you find some details?			
How do the quotes show what people felt and thought?			

writing guides

Photocopiable

Comparing news

● Choose four different news stories. Number them 1 to 4 and answer these questions for each story.

What works well in the first part	What the story might be about	Question(s) answered in the first sentence	The two most striking words in the headline

Illustration © 2002, Michael Rees

In the news

 Think why the story will interest readers.

 Answer the questions:
Who? What? When? Where? Why?

 Give the story a snappy
and striking headline.

 Make sure you pack in all the details.

 Use quotes from people,
showing what they saw and thought.

 Don't use too many words.

 Make the story interesting.

Section 2
Developing writing

In this section, children build on their news-writing skills, developing the features of news stories that were identified in section 1.

Resources

As you work through this section, there are some vital resources that you will need in your classroom. The first is a steady supply of real newspapers: if you can, order a daily newspaper if your class doesn't already receive one. Mix the styles of newspaper such as broadsheet and tabloid; local and national.

A variety of other news resources is also useful. This could involve listening to radio bulletins or watching lunchtime news on the television. There should be space on the classroom wall for children to put up selected news stories. Take note of things happening in the school or community to provide worthwhile news material, such as school holidays, visits, trips, meetings of the Governors and so on.

Building on good examples

The activities in this section build on the features of news reporting that were summarised on the poster at the end of section 1. There is a consideration of what makes for an interesting story, followed by activities that look at the sorts of questions to be asked, answers to be given and quotes to be used. It is useful to keep referring back to the poster for support and constant reminders about 'facts and quotes'.

Different views

This section also teases out the issue of different views on an event, a vital component of news reporting. Read any newspaper and it should demonstrate the fact that one event can be seen in a number of ways.

Bringing writing to life

When making notes, it adds excitement if you encourage the children to use reporter's notepads, and to study real news to help make their writing purposeful and realistic.

Activity 1: Morning conference

Objective

Identify features that writers use to provoke readers' reactions (Year 3 Strand 8).

What to do

The first task of journalism is to find breaking news. This activity involves children in that idea.

● Organise the class to work in groups of four. Explain to the children that they are going to hold a 'morning conference' as if they are reporters working on a local newspaper. Explain that in these meetings stories are discussed, in order to decide what needs to be found out as part of the reporting process.

● Hand out photocopiable page 25 'Morning conference', which contains a series of notes about stories they could cover. Tell them that they can only cover half of these. Which ones would they cover and why? Ask them to cut out their choices and sort them into ones they definitely would, might and definitely would not cover – but stipulate that only five can remain.

● Note down questions around the children's chosen stories. Ask them to write a one-sentence summary of each story, then, as a group, think of four things they would need to find out about each news item.

Activity 2: First sentence

Objective

Make decisions about form and purpose, identify success criteria and use them to evaluate writing (Year 3 Strand 9).

What's on the CD-ROM

First sentence
● Text entry activity, enabling children to gather and compare facts.

Media resources
● 'Policing' image to display and discuss.

What to do

This lesson focuses on the first line of a news story as the first sentence is sometimes all the reader gets through.

● Open the activity 'First sentence' on the CD-ROM. Explain to the children that the secret of a good news story is to answer the key questions: Who? What? When? Where? Why?

● Tell them you are going to focus on opening sentences. These should get straight to the five key questions.

● Show the children the 'Policing' photo from the 'Media resources' section of the CD-ROM and ask them to think of an opening sentence. For example: The police (who) were called yesterday (when) to Sheffington town centre, (where) where a riot broke out (what) after a demonstration by local farmers.

● Point out that the example above answers four of the five key questions (we don't know why the farmers were demonstrating) and if necessary, the rest of the story could be cut (as often happens in a real newspaper where space is short) and it would still make sense.

● Using news stories the children have come across, ask them to complete the CD-ROM activity or photocopiable page 26, then share some examples of their opening sentences.

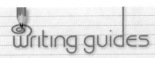

Activity 3: What did they say?

Objective

Empathise with characters and debate moral dilemmas portrayed in texts (Year 3 Strand 8).

What's on the CD-ROM

What did they say?
- Text entry activity, where children write their own quotes to use in news writing.

Media resources
- Image of 'Reporters' to display and discuss.

What to do

This lesson focuses on quotes and how they give insight into people's reactions, opinions and feelings in a news story.

- Show the children the 'Reporters' image from the 'Media resources' section of the CD-ROM. Ask them what they think the person talking to the reporters might be feeling and how they might be talking. Explain that news reporters often have to capture peoples' feelings about an event.

- Display the activity 'What did they say' from the CD-ROM. Ask the children to think about the story that is unfolding. Can they suggest who the different participants are, what is happening and how they might be reacting?

- In pairs, ask the children to think what each character may be saying, and to fill in the speech bubbles on screen or on photocopiable page 27. Ask them to suggest how these speech bubbles might be incorporated into a news story.

- Invite the children to read out some of their quotes; can the rest of the class guess who said the quote? Discuss any feelings and opinions conveyed by the quotes.

- On another sheet of paper, tell the children to put these quotes into sentences, punctuated with speech marks, as they would appear in a news report. Share some of their sentences when they have finished.

Activity 4: It's a fact

Objective

Identify and summarise evidence from a text to support a hypothesis (Year 4 Strand 7).

What's on the CD-ROM

It's a fact
- Drag and drop activity to explore the differences between facts and opinions.

What to do

Use this lesson to help distinguish between facts and opinions within news stories.

- Split the board into two columns headed 'Fact' and 'Opinion'. Make some statements that are facts ('The door is green') and some that are opinions ('Cheese tastes nice'). Decide whether each statement is one that everyone could agree with (fact) or one that some people might disagree with (opinion); write the sentences in the appropriate columns.

- Explain that good journalism relies on telling a story through the reporting of facts, rather than opinion that can be disagreed with.

- Open the CD-ROM activity 'It's a fact' and ask the children to sort the statements into the categories 'Fact' or 'Opinion'. Some children may prefer to use the photocpiable page 28. Ask the children how they knew which statements were fact and which were opinion.

- Hand out a selection of short newspaper articles and working in groups encourage the children to see if they can pick out the facts and opinions in them. Discuss the articles with the class.

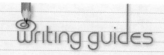

Activity 5: Question generator

Objective

Make decisions about form and purpose, identify success criteria and use them to evaluate writing (Year 3 Strand 9).

What's on the CD-ROM

Question generator
● Text entry activity to help develop good questions.

Media resources
● 'Accident scene' image to display and discuss.

What to do

Asking questions is an important part of gathering news. This lesson focuses on developing the skill of asking questions as a reporter or journalist.

● Recall some news stories that the children have seen on television or in newspapers recently.

● Display the 'Accident scene' image from the 'Media resources' section of the CD-ROM, and together think of questions you could ask about the event or the people involved. Open the activity 'Question generator' from the CD-ROM and working in groups, ask the children to type in questions about the photograph. Write the first word or words of each question on the board, for example: 'When was...?' 'Why did...?' 'What happened...?' Point out some of the question words that are commonly appearing.

● Hand out copies of photocopiable page 29 'Question generator' and working individually, ask the children to think of questions surrounding a particular news story of their choice. Explain that they should write eight questions they could ask if they were investigating the story, based on the sentence starters on the board and around the page. Challenge the children to use a different sentence starter for each question.

Activity 6: What did you think?

Objective

Deduce characters' reasons for behaviour from their actions and explain how ideas are developed in non-fiction texts (Year 4 Strand 7).

What's on the CD-ROM

Media resources
● The 'Reporters' image provides an opportunity for children to infer thoughts and feelings from an image.

What to do

This activity encourages children to gather the reactions to an event – an integral part of communicating news.

● Display the 'Reporters' image from the 'Media resources' section of the CD-ROM and remind the children that reporters need to capture the feelings surrounding an event.

● Choose a school event (the school play or a football match, for example) on which various people could comment. Invite the children to think of people they could ask to comment on the event (perhaps staff, parents or children from another class) and what questions they would want to ask these people.

● Ask pairs of children to approach one person from their list for a comment and, as they listen to what their interviewee says, to take notes.

● Tell them to record the responses they get on photocopiable page 30 'What do you think?', looking at the words provided for potential sentence starters, for example, 'Ms Martin wondered...'.

● Invite the children to write up the story in shared or guided writing, drawing on the best examples of opinion gathered from the roving reporters.

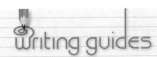

Activity 7: One event, two views

Objective

Deduce characters' reasons for behaviour from their actions and explain how ideas are developed in non-fiction texts (Year 4 Strand 7).

What's on the CD-ROM

One event, two views
- Text entry activity to record different points of view.

What to do

There is never one, simple view of an event, and good news reporting teases out the range of views that can be taken of one story – this is a gem of an activity that investigates different viewpoints.

- Ask the children to think of some situations in which different people can have different points of view (for example, someone telling somebody off, someone who thinks their neighbour's hedge is too high or a child being told they can't have a pet).

- Open the activity 'One event, two views' from the CD-ROM. Tell the children to choose an event and complete the rest of the activity on screen. The children should record the different thoughts people might have about the same event. Try this again but with a different chosen event.

- Using photocopiable page 31 'One event, two views', ask the children to come up with two other examples of events that prompt divergent views. The children could base the events on particular news stories they have read; remind them to think of possible different points of view taken by the people involved in those events. They should then complete the rest of the sheet by thinking of possible sentences, quoting what each person might have said that could be incorporated into a news story.

Activity 8: Quoted or reported?

Objective

Make decisions about form and purpose, identify success criteria and use them to evaluate writing (Year 3 Strand 9).

What to do

This lesson looks at the way news stories present direct and reported speech.

- Play the children a news bulletin, either a podcast from the Internet or the radio. Ask them to listen carefully and to make a note of sentences spoken by people who are interviewed.

- Once the bulletin has ended, write one of the sentences on the board, as direct speech, for example: 'Mr Palmer said "I was amazed,"' then explain to the children that this could also be written as reported speech in which the words are not quoted: 'Mr Palmer said he was amazed'.

- Point out the use of first- and third-person speech respectively in each example. Ask the children to turn some of the quotes from their notes into reported speech.

- Using photocopiable page 32 'Quoted or reported', ask the children to match the direct and reported speech captions in a series of comments from the owner of the flower shop in the scene on photocopiable page 27 'What did they say?'.

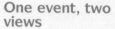

Activity 9: Write your own headline

Objective

Identify features that writers use to provoke readers' reactions (Year 3 Strand 8).

What's on the CD-ROM

Write your own headline
- Text entry activity to create own headlines.

What to do

Use this lesson to investigate headlines. Headlines are one of the aspects of news writing that can be really good fun – they encourage drama, wordplay and enjoyment!

- Begin by looking at a range of news stories, asking the children how they think the stories got their headlines. What connection is there between the headline and the story? Look for examples of puns and wordplay in headlines.

- Having looked at a range of headlines, tell the children that they are going to try to create their own. Display the activity 'Write your own headline' on the CD-ROM and together read the stories.

- Using one as an example, gather some suggestions for potential headlines, drawing on puns ('Scary Dog Tale') and promoting drama ('Freak Wave Fears!').

- Ask the children to complete the on-screen activity in small groups or fill in photocopiable page 33. They need to think of a headline for each story and write it in the space provided. At the end of the session, share their ideas and choose the best headlines created.

Activity 10: Standfirst

Objective

Identify how different texts are organised, including reference texts, magazines and leaflets, on paper and on screen (Year 3 Strand 7).

What to do

This lesson investigates the use of standfirsts in news reports.

- Show the children some examples from newspapers of a standfirst. This is normally directly underneath the main headline, and provides more information about the story than the headline. For example, a headline 'Dinosaur lives!' might have a standfirst such as 'Scientists thaw out giant lizards', which would be written in larger type than the actual story but smaller than the headline.

- From your collection of newspapers, ask the children to look for and identify standfirsts. Share these with the class.

- Ask the children to look through photocopiable page 34 'Standfirst', in which the news stories have headlines and first sentences. What standfirsts would they write for each of these?

- Think of some news stories for which children could write their own standfirst. Remind them that they need to start with a few details that they want to capture and a lot of words, and then narrow these down to ideally as many words as they have fingers on one hand, counting off as they say it aloud. They can slip in another word or two, but two hands worth of fingers is a no-no!

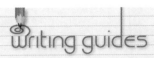

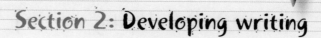
Morning conference

● You are a team of reporters with the *Sheffington News*. Which five stories from this pile would you investigate, and why?

A dog is trapped down a disused tunnel.

A coach of elderly people on a day trip has got completely lost – no-one knows where it is. No contact. Nothing.

The local secondary school, Dunkirk Road, is putting on a performance of 'Grease'.

The Queen is visiting Emmfield School, a primary school in the area.

There's been a robbery at a pet shop on Sheffington High Street.

Gladys, the rhino at Sheffington Zoo, has given birth to a baby rhino.

The huge 'Buy-It' supermarket in Sheffington is five years old today.

Louis Dylan, from Sheffington, has been arrested on suspicion of arson.

A woman at Sheffington Hospital has given birth to quintupulets.

Jack Flaps, businessman in Sheffington, says he's had a mountain on the moon named after him.

First sentence

- Choose three news stories and use the grid below to help you note down some key facts about each story. Then try to write an opening sentence for each story that answers each of the key questions.

Who?	What?	When?	Where?	Opening sentence

Illustrations © 2002, Michael Rees

What did they say?

- Look at this scene and think about what each of the people might be saying. Write your ideas in the speech bubbles.

Illustrations © 2002, Michael Rees

It's a fact

● Sort these statements into ones that are facts (things that are known to be true) and ones that are opinions (things people could discuss and disagree with).

Spiders are scary	Chelsea is the best football team	Mount Everest is the world's tallest mountain
Our school is the best one around	Two plus two equals four	PE is more fun than art
A spider has eight legs	It's healthy to clean your teeth	The Earth is a sphere
Bread tastes better when it's toasted	Bread is made from flour	Grass is green

Illustrations © 2002, Michael Rees

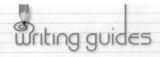

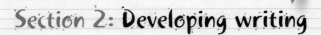

Question generator

● Imagine you are going to write a news story. What would you want to find out? Write the title of the story in the middle wheel. Think of some questions you could answer when writing your story, and write these in the cogs. Try to use different words to start each question – the ideas around the page might help you.

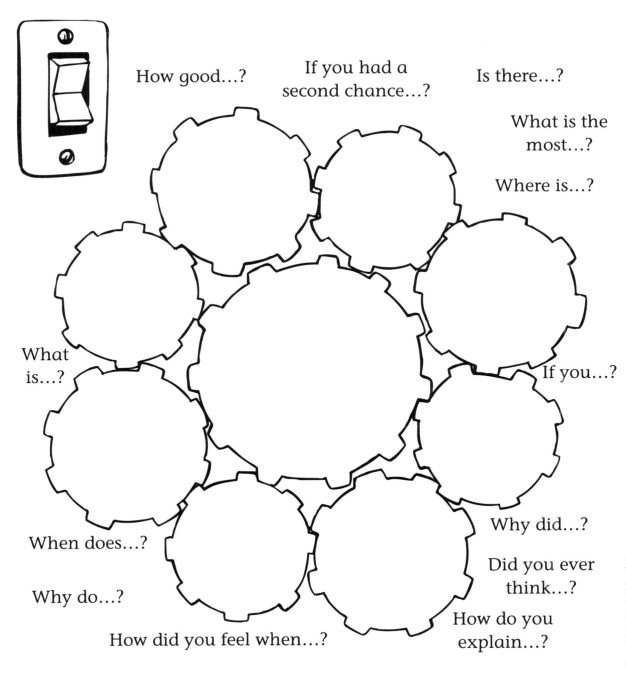

How good...?

If you had a second chance...?

Is there...?

What is the most...?

Where is...?

What is...?

If you...?

When does...?

Why did...?

Did you ever think...?

Why do...?

How did you feel when...?

How do you explain...?

Illustrations © 2002, Michael Rees

What did you think?

● Write down what people thought about the event.

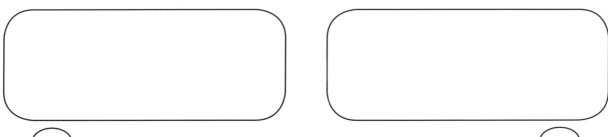

Illustrations © 2010, Michael Rees

writing guides

One event, two views

- Two people can think very different things about the same event.
- Use the thought bubbles below to show how two people might have different thoughts about the same event.

Event

Person 1

Person 2

Event

Person 1

Person 2

Illustrations © 2002, Michael Rees

Quoted or reported?

● Cut out the boxes below and match the direct quotes
Ms Flowers said with sentences that report her comments.
Be careful – some of them are very similar!

Ms Flowers said she was amazed to see an alligator in the street.	"Everyone was pleased" Ms Flowers bubbled, "We'd love to see another."
Ms Flowers said it was rare to see alligators outside of a zoo.	"I was quite unnerved at the sight," Ms Flowers shuddered, recalling the alligator.
Ms Flowers was pleased to see the alligator in the street and says they'd be happy to see another.	"It isn't often folks round here see real, live alligators," Ms Flowers explained. "They were thrilled."
Ms Flowers observed lots of people were thrilled at the sight of a real, live alligator.	"What? An alligator? In the street? Goodness me!" a stunned Ms Flowers exclaimed. "Whatever next? "
The alligator clearly scared Ms Flowers. She said it was an unnerving experience.	"You don't see alligators that often," Ms Flowers observed, "At least, not outside of a zoo."
Ms Flowers was surprised to hear an alligator had walked past her shop, having missed the whole event.	Ms Flowers said "I was amazed to see an alligator in the street"

Illustration © 2010, Michael Rees

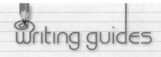

writing guides

Write your own headline

● Try to write a headline for each of these stories.

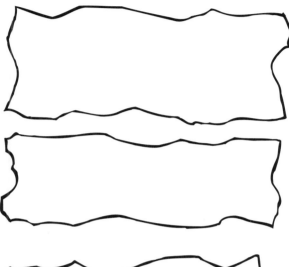

Giant waves have been crashing along the south coast. Freak waves, some topping a massive 10 metres, have caused havoc in seaside resorts.

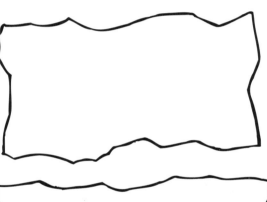

Toodles, the most frightened dog in Britain, is scared of his own tail. The poodle runs yelping if he catches sight of it.

Jan Froome of Essex passed her driving test yesterday at the hundredth attempt. Ms Froome has paid a total of £3000 on lessons and has been learning for 20 years. "I never thought I'd make it," a delighted Jan told reporters.

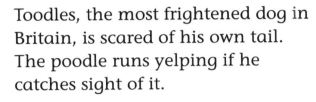

A baby rhino, Bubbles, has been born at Chessfield Zoo. This is the first rhino born at the zoo.

Children at a London school yesterday arrived to find their teachers were not there. A mix-up had occurred and the teachers were away on a training event. Mum Maureen Fowl commented "It all seemed so quiet we all went home."

A new Christmas card has been invented with a built-in camera that records the words and faces of anyone opening it.

Standfirst

- Add the standfirsts to these stories.

WHAT A TIP

_____

_____

Taxi driver Sid Cole was amazed to find £30,000 left in his taxi after a busy day's work.

Freeze peas

_____

_____

Children at an Essex primary school were served frozen peas that hadn't been defrosted or cooked.

Monkey Business

_____

_____

A shopkeeper, awoken in the night by noises downstairs in his shop, found an escaped chimpanzee was playing with the till.

BAKER LEAVES HIS DOUGH

_____

_____

A secret millionaire baker from Surrey, with no living relatives, left £30 million in his will to his old primary school.

LAPTOP FROM THE TOP

_____

_____

Businesswoman Cheryl Parker was amazed to find her laptop worked after falling from the top floor of her office block.

MIND THE STEP

_____

_____

A builder in Watford realized his firm had completed building four houses, but hadn't put stairs in any of them.

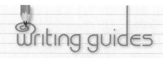

Section 3

Writing

Drawing on the features of news stories discussed in section 2, this section guides the children through the process of producing their own news story. The scenarios presented in the first two projects guide children to firstly look at the way an event is presented through a range of perspectives and how their job, as reporters, is to capture these in one story.

The news-writing process

The activities are designed to model the process of news gathering, drawing on scenarios that need transforming into written reports. The details that enhance each report such as the process of gathering information and quotes is built up through simulated news stories. These are then turned into structured news reports. The modelling of the news-writing process is vital, because news gathering and writing isn't just as straightforward as sitting down and writing a text.

These projects should give children a sense of the enjoyment to be gained from being a news reporter. Any use of reporters' notebooks, flipcharts and enjoying playing at being a real journalist will only serve to enhance the process.

The projects

The first project draws out the notion of different perspectives and views; when tackling these, your role is to be provocative in enouraging the children to think of things characters could say that haven't yet been thought up.

The second project is the one that most closely models the experience a reporter has in combining different elements into one report. It takes one incident – a pet shop robbery – and presents children with a set of statements and sources from which they can compile a news story. As they piece these together they should tease out the underlying plot – that the robbers made a mess of a bank robbery – because the the bank was shut!

In the third project, children are given material with which to construct the front page of their own newspaper; this can be done as a screen activity or by hand using the photocopiable sheets provided. It might be a good idea to encourage the children to complete the activty on the CD-ROM and also on paper because the cut-and-stick nature of this task is important; the children need to engage with the physical task of constructing the front page.

Writing tips

Throughout this section, remind the children of the following tips developed in sections 1 and 2.
- Ask why a reader would be interested in the story.
- Use snappy and interesting headlines.
- Make the most of the story's opening.
- Provide details the reader will want to know.
- Think up questions that the story will need to answer.
- Include quotes and opinions from those involved in the story.

Project 1: News scenarios

Objectives

Infer characters' feelings in fiction and consequences in logical explanations (Year 3 Strand 7). Empathise with characters and debate moral dilemmas portrayed in texts (Year 3 Strand 8). Deduce characters' reasons for behaviour from their actions and explain how ideas are developed in non-fiction texts (Year 4 Strand 7).

What's on the CD-ROM

News scenarios
● Two news scenarios to base news reports on. Children type in questions about the scenarios to help with the news story write up.

My news story
● Write a news report based on one of the news scenarios investigated in the lesson.

What to do

To develop news stories we need to begin with a scenario or a situation. This lesson provides two scenarios that give rise to a set of questions and resultant news stories.

● Ask the children to look through the storyboard on photocopiable page 38 'News scenario 1', thinking through questions such as: 'Why would this make a good news story?'; 'What is interesting about this scenario?'

● Open the activity 'News scenarios' on the CD-ROM. Ask the children to look at 'News scenario 1' and type in a set of questions about it. Tell them to think about the participants in the story and to give them names, this will help with discussion and with the writing of the news story.

● Working in pairs, with notebooks, tell the children to role-play this scenario, with individuals pretending to be the woman with the dog, her friend, the crane operator or the child. What questions would a news reporter put to these characters? What answers would they give?

● Look at 'News scenario 2' on the CD-ROM and give out individual copies of photocopiable page 39. Ask the children to follow the same process, but with greater independence. They should figure out the scenario and type in their questions on screen; they should move on to conducting interviews and gathering some notes. Remind the children that the friends of the cyclist and the driver are very important witnesses and can also give some feeling to the story.

● Once the children have their questions for 'News scenario 2' ask each pair of reporters to meet with another pair to compare their questions and any thoughts they may have about the answers.

● When the children are satisfied with their notes and questions from the two scenarios, they should be in a position to write up one of the two stories, giving the main facts and quotes from those involved.

● Tell the children to select one of the writing templates from the CD-ROM (click on the 'My news story' button to access these.) Explain that they are to choose one of the scenarios and write their news report into a template. Alternatively, the templates can be printed out if the children wish to write their reports by hand.

● Before writing their reports, remind the children to work out details, such as the names of the participants, their ages, where they were heading when the incident occurred and so on. They will also need to think of comments and quotes from the participants, expressing their thoughts and feelings.

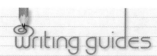

Project 2: Burglary!

Objective

Summarise and shape material and ideas from different sources to write convincing and informative non-narrative texts (Year 4 Strand 9).

What's on the CD-ROM

Burglary!
- Roll over the texts to reveal questions.

Media resources
- Audio file 'Police statement'.

My news story
- Choose a template to write a report.

What to do

In this lesson the children act like real reporters; they are given an open-ended scenario which allows them to gather details from which they can later write their report.

- Tell the children that everyone is to think and behave like a reporter. News has just come in of a robbery on Sheffington High Street; a pet shop has been robbed.

- Explain that reporters often have to make quick, short notes when listening to a police or witness statement about an event. Listen to the audio clip 'Police statement' from the 'Media resources' section of the CD-ROM; they should jot down as many facts and details as possible in their notebooks as they listen.

- As a class, scan through and discuss the different texts on photocopiable pages 40 and 41 'Burglary'. Encourage the children to jot down short details and list any questions they may have.

- Display the activity 'Burglary!' on the CD-ROM. Roll over the texts to reveal various questions about the burglary. Do the children have similar questions? Encourage them to suggest some possible answers.

- Tell the children to write a draft of their stories, then to produce a real news report using their chosen template from the 'My news story' section on the CD-ROM .

Project 3: News stories

Objectives

Summarise and shape material and ideas from different sources to write convincing and informative non-narrative texts (Year 4 Strand 9).

What's on the CD-ROM

Media resources
- All four images to display and discuss.

News story planner
- Plan a newspaper front page.

My news story
- Create a front page using the templates.

What to do

This project allows the children to develop aspects of news layout such as the headline, standfirst, byline, caption and quote.

- Display the four images from the 'Media resources' section of the CD-ROM. Ask: *Would any of these make good front-page stories?*

- In small groups, ask them to make up two news stories they could report on. Give them the freedom to make up facts and quotes.

- Open the 'News story planner' on the CD-ROM. Tell the children to think of a headline, standfirst, byline (who the article is by), caption and quote for one of the stories. They can upload their own picture or photo. This activity will help them to create a newspaper front page.

- Ask the children to choose the 'front page' templates from the 'My news story' section on the CD-ROM to write their actual front page. The front page template is split into two templates, these can be printed out and joined together.

- Some of the children my prefer to work on photocopiable pages 42 and 43, where they will need to cut out the templates (on page 42) and stick them onto the columns on (page 43).

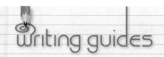

News scenario 1

Questions

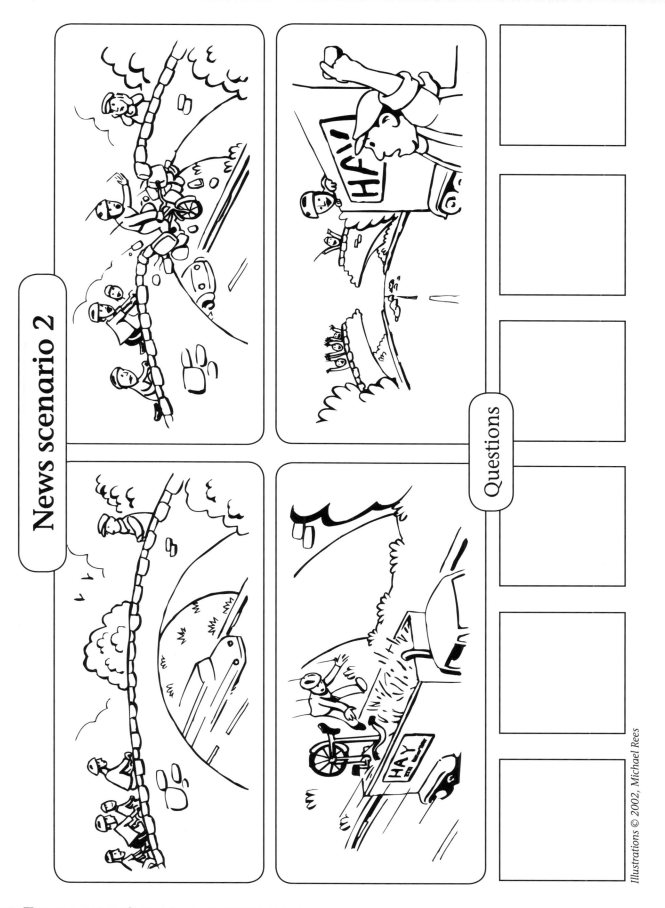

Burglary!

● A burglary has been committed in the High Street, Sheffington. You are a reporter for the *Sheffington Daily News*. Use these materials to compile a story.

From: News Desk / **To:** Ace Reporter / **Sent:** Wednesday 15 February, 13:50

Subject: Robbery at Pet Shop in High St Sheffington

Two robbers escaped with money and 12 tins of cat food.

Please investigate.

Police statement

At 12.55 today a robbery occurred on High Street, Sheffington. A blue Forxhall car pulled up alongside Shoppo's supermarket on High Street. One woman left the car and entered the pet shop in Sheffington. The suspect reached over the counter and pulled money from the till. The suspect also took a cardboard carton, containing 12 tins of cat food. She then returned to the car and drove south, along Broomspring Lane. The pet shop owner, Mr Alan Gerbil, was injured as he gave chase.

Eyewitness 1: Molly Swan, age 40

I am a solicitor and was on my lunch break at the time. The car came along the road and screeched to a halt outside Shoppo's. I was just walking out of the shop. The man in the car shouted, "I think it's shut, you twit!" and the woman got out of the car and shouted, "We're here now." So she ran over the road. She had long red hair. She went and stopped in front of the bank, then ran into the pet shop. When she came out again she ran over the road and dived into the car. The man shouted, "That was a waste of time! We haven't even got a cat!" and then they drove away really fast down the road.

Illustrations © 2002, Michael Rees

Interview with shopkeeper

Q: What happened when the robber entered the shop?

A: She comes running in and stood in that doorway. She looked around and then saw the till. Before I could close it she leaned over really quickly and took the money.

Q: Did anyone try to stop her?

A: There was nobody else in the shop. I moved towards her and she picked up one of the heavy trays of cat food tins. It looked as if she was going to chuck it at me. So I stepped back and off she ran.

Q: Did anything else happen?

A: When she grabbed the cat food a big pile of tins wobbled, then after a bit they fell over.

Q: How did you feel when she entered the shop?

A: I was scared. She looked really wild. I thought, "I didn't go in to pet sales for this."

Q: Did you go after her?

A: I did, but I fell over all the cans of pet food. That was when I twisted my ankle and I couldn't chase the robber.

Eyewitness 2: Hanif Raja, age 28

I was on my way back to work in the supermarket. I had just turned into the High Street and the next thing I knew this woman comes running across the road. It was a long way down the street but it looked like she went and tried the door of the bank, then ran into the pet shop. It looked a bit suspicious so I ran down towards the bank. I got there and tried the door. It was locked. I was about to go into the pet shop and see Mr Gerbil when the door opened and out ran this woman. She had really scary eyes and she threw a tin of cat food at me. It hit my head and I was knocked unconscious.

Questions raised at discussion with editor

- What did the robbers actually do?
- Why didn't someone stop them?
- Why would anyone rob a pet shop?

Illustrations © 2002, Michael Rees

Photocopiable **SCHOLASTIC**
www.scholastic.co.uk

News stories

- Use this template to make the front page of a newspaper. Design a title for your newspaper and stick it over this space, then fill the other spaces with different features of a news story. You will need to include:

a **picture** for one of your stories

a short **picture** caption

another headline for your second story

a **headline** that draws attention to the story, for example 'ALLIGATOR ESCAPES'

a **standfirst** with a bit more about the story, such as 'Zoo Loses Dangerous Creature in Town'

a **byline**, with the name of the reporter

a **quote** from an interviewee

Section 4

Review

Assessing writing

News writing involves a constant need for self-editing. Reporters have certain goals and deadlines, as well as word counts. So it is possible in this type of writing to make the assessment a part of the excitement of shaping up both children's writing and their expertise at the job. It is also often a collaborative exercise, so children will find this a good opportunity to share in the assessment of each other's work.

Self review and Peer review

Photocopiable page 45 'Self review' provides some questions for the children to consider when reflecting on their own work, and will focus their attention on paricular features of a news story. Encourage them to complete a copy of the sheet for each story they write, so they can see how their writing is progressing.

Having written a number of stories, the children could look at refining one in the light of what they have done well in another. If, for example, they used quotes well in one story but another had a better opening sentence, they could combine these elements in improving one of the stories.

A good news story satisfies the reader's curiosity. The 'Peer review' activity on photocopiable page 46 allows children to swap stories and check that four of the reader's key questions have been covered in the writing. This could be done as a shared task, working in pairs to look together at a story, or swapping stories with one another first and then completing the sheet individually.

Teacher review

The Assessing Pupil's Progress approach provides a means of regularly reviewing children's work against national standards. In writing, the assessment focus is based on the National Curriculum Programmes of Study, and the level descriptions provide a detailed assessment framework to assess teaching and learning in all aspects of writing.

Carrying out an overall review of each child's progress and attainment will enable you to evaluate the progress children make towards specific learning goals, set group and individual learning targets, and ensure the next steps are planned at an appropriate level. The review may also highlight gaps in teaching and learning.

Use the table on photocopiable page 47 'Teacher review' to assess children's progress and attainment at the end of a unit. It enables you to relate a child's finished piece of writing to the Assessing Pupil's Progress guidelines for writing. The indicators will help you judge which level the child is closest to in each Assessment Focus (AF).

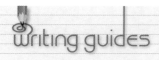

Self review

- After you have written a news story, look back at your work and answer the following questions.

Who will be interested in this story?	
What is the most important word in your headline?	
What are the three most significant details in the story?	
Why did you use one of your quotes?	

Peer review

● Ask a friend to read one of your stories, and to see whether they can tell you:

who is in the story

_____

_____

_____

what the story is about

_____

_____

_____

when the story happened

_____

_____

_____

where the events took place

_____

_____

_____

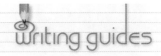
writing guides

Teacher review

Child's name: _____   Date: _____

	AF5 Vary sentences for clarity, purpose and effect.	AF4 Construct paragraphs and use cohesion within and between paragraphs.	AF1 Write imaginative, interesting and thoughtful texts.	AF2 Produce texts which are appropriate to task, reader and purpose.
LEVEL 2	Sentence openings use the 'who, what, when, where' etc structure. Generally consistent use of past tense sentences to relate news reports of events.	Ideas grouped into sections.	Content is relevant to chosen news story. Brief suggestion of viewpoints taken by those involved in news story.	Basic news telling purpose established. Some use of headlines.
LEVEL 3	Opening sentence relates main points of story, with variety in others, such as those delivering quotations. Past events related through consistent use of past tense verb forms, not always secure.	News story structured into paragraphs/sections.	Appropriate ideas and content make up the body of the report. Some elaboration on basic events.	Purpose of news recount established. Headline, first sentence and quotation use established.
LEVEL 4	Variety in sentence length, structure and subject. Accurate and consistent use of past tense and verb forms when reporting events.	Paragraphs/sections used in planning and writing to organise news content.	Relevant material and facts chosen for inclusion in news story. Viewpoint varies between reporter's distance and quotes of those involved.	Main purpose of news reportage is clear. Headline, quotation and news reporting style are appropriate to purpose.

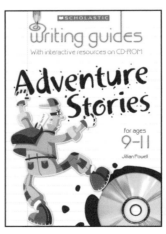